W9-CZX-203

Mar11–DPA

This item no longer
belongs to Davenport
Public Library

HOPKINS PUBLIC LIBRARY
DAVENPORT, IOWA

DAVENPORT PUBLIC LIBRARY
321 MAIN STREET
DAVENPORT, IOWA 52801

STRANGE *but* TRUE SPORTS

BY LORI POLYDOROS

Reading Consultant:
Barbara J. Fox
Reading Specialist
North Carolina State University

CAPSTONE PRESS
a capstone imprint

Blazers is published by Capstone Press,
151 Good Counsel Drive, P.O. Box 669, Mankato, Minnesota 56002.
www.capstonepub.com

Copyright © 2011 by Capstone Press, a Capstone imprint.
All rights reserved.
No part of this publication may be reproduced in whole or in part, or stored in a retrieval system,
or transmitted in any form or by any means, electronic, mechanical, photocopying, recording,
or otherwise, without written permission of the publisher.
For information regarding permission, write to Capstone Press,
151 Good Counsel Drive, P.O. Box 669, Dept. R, Mankato, Minnesota 56002.
Printed in the United States of America in North Mankato, Minnesota.
032010
005740CGF10

Books published by Capstone Press are manufactured with paper
containing at least 10 percent post-consumer waste.

Library of Congress Cataloging-in-Publication Data
Polydoros, Lori, 1968–
  Strange but true sports / by Lori Polydoros.
    p. cm. — (Blazers. Strange but true)
  Includes bibliographical references and index.
  Summary: "Describes unusual sports and their strange rules, locations, and competitors"—
Provided by publisher.
  ISBN 978-1-4296-4550-8 (library binding)
  1. Sports—Miscellanea—Juvenile literature. I. Title. II. Series.
  GV707.P585 2011
  796—dc22   2009050388

Editorial Credits
Editor: Kathryn Clay
Designer: Kyle Grenz
Media Researcher: Svetlana Zhurkin
Production Specialist: Laura Manthe

Photo Credits
Alamy/Barry Bland, 6–7; Buzz Pictures, 22–23; Jack Sullivan, 4–5, 12–13
Corbis/Aurora Photos/Harrison Shull, 18–19; Colin McPherson, 24–25; Jeremy Horner,
    10–11; Patrick Ward, 8–9
Getty Images/Bongarts/Lars Baron, 20–21; Chris McGrath, 28–29; Richard Heathcote,
    cover, 16–17
Matthew Clay, 26–27
Shutterstock/Andrejs Pidjass, cover (texture); Chris Turner, 14–15

TABLE OF CONTENTS

The STRANGER the BETTER

Globe riders roll downhill inside huge plastic balls. Hockey players hold their breath to score underwater goals. Some people chase after cheese. **Competitors** around the world play strange sports.

competitor—a person who is trying to win a sport or game

stick

puck

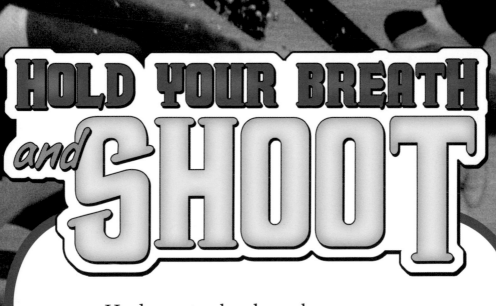

HOLD YOUR BREATH and SHOOT

Underwater hockey players wear masks and fins. Players use mini hockey sticks. They shoot pucks into underwater goals. Players try to score before running out of breath.

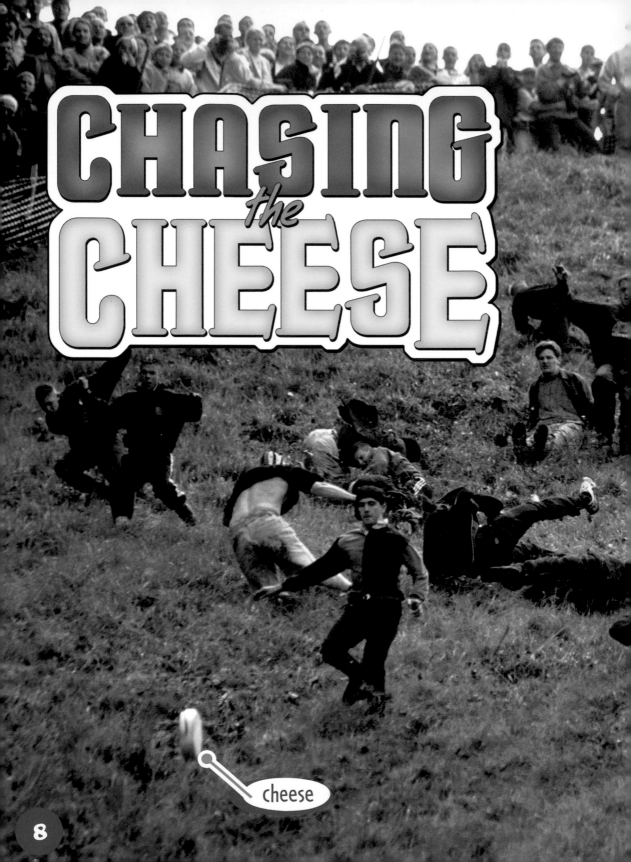

CHASING *the* CHEESE

cheese

STRANGE but TRUE

Cheese can roll downhill up to 70 miles (113 kilometers) per hour.

People in England race downhill after cheese. Chasing cheese can be dangerous. People tumble down steep hills. They get scrapes, bruises, and broken bones.

9

ELEPHANT POLO

Most **polo** players ride horses. But in Asia, people play elephant polo. Elephant polo isn't easy. Sometimes the ball gets stuck in piles of poop.

polo—a game played by two teams of four players; the players try to hit a small ball using long, wooden mallets

polo ball

READY, SET, EAT

Competitive eaters stuff stinging **nettles** into their mouths. Eaters must keep the burning leaves in their stomachs. Throwing up means losing!

nettle—a weed with sharp, stinging hairs

stinging nettles

STRANGE but TRUE

Some people say stinging nettles taste like a mix of spinach and cow poop.

GLOBE RIDING

STRANGE *but* TRUE

The fastest globe rider rolled downhill at 32 miles (51 kilometers) per hour.

Imagine riding inside a giant hamster ball. Since 1990, people have been rolling downhill inside clear plastic globes. Globe riders twist and turn all the way down.

SLIMY SNORKELING

Bog snorkelers wear flippers and **snorkels** to slosh through muddy water. Swimmers battle weeds and leeches. The fastest swimmer wins.

bog—a wet, spongy area of land

snorkel—a tube that you use to breath through when you are swimming under water

snorkel

More than 200 people compete in bog snorkeling each year.

ONE-WHEELED WONDERS

Off-road **unicycles** have wide tires to handle bumps. Riders pedal over grass, ice, and snow. They hop over rocks and slip through small spaces.

unicycle—a vehicle that has pedals like a bicycle but only one wheel and no handlebars

One extreme cyclist pedaled on the Great Wall of China.

unicycle

CHESS BOXING

Chess boxing combines a strong mind and a strong body. A player can win with a **checkmate**. Or a player can land a **knockout** to win.

checkmate—a chess move that ends the game

knockout—a victory in which a fighter's opponent is unable to get up after being knocked to the ground

STRANGE *but* TRUE

One extreme ironer set up his board in Antarctica. He ironed in temperatures of -47 degrees Fahrenheit (-44 degrees Celsius).

IRONING to the MAX

Here's a twist on a boring chore. Competitors look for extreme places to iron. These wacky athletes iron in trees and on trampolines. They even iron while hanging from cliffs.

CALLING *all* WORMS

Worm charmers use **vibrations** to get worms out of the ground. They bang drums or sing songs. To win, charmers must catch the most worms in 30 minutes.

vibration—a fast movement back and forth

STRANGE but TRUE

The world record for worm charming is 567 worms in 30 minutes.

RACING PUMPKINS

Pumpkins aren't just for making pies. Giant pumpkins are turned into boats. Racers hollow out the pumpkins and attach boat motors. Racers fight to keep their pumpkins above water.

STRANGE but TRUE

Some racers reach speeds of 6 miles (10 kilometers) per hour.

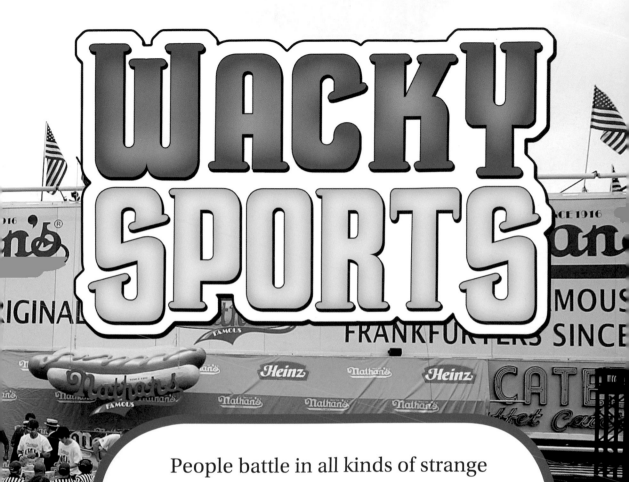

WACKY SPORTS

People battle in all kinds of strange sports. Some hope to bring visitors to their town. Others just like an odd challenge. Whatever their reason, they are sure to draw a crowd of curious fans.

GLOSSARY

bog (BAHG)—a wet, spongy area of land

checkmate (CHEK-mayt)—a chess move that ends the game

competitor (kuhm-PE-tuh-tuhr)—a person who is trying to win a sport or game

knockout (NOK-out)—a victory in which a fighter's opponent is unable to get up after being knocked to the ground

nettle (NET-uhl)—a weed with sharp, stinging hairs

polo (POH-loh)—a game played by two teams of four players; the players try to hit a small ball using long, wooden mallets

snorkel (SNOR-kuhl)—a tube that you use to breathe through when you are swimming under water

unicycle (YOO-nuh-sye-kuhl)—a vehicle that has pedals like a bicycle but only one wheel and no handlebars

vibration (vye-BRAY-shuhn)—a fast movement back and forth

READ MORE

Abraham, Philip. *Extreme Sports Stars*. Sports Stars. New York: Children's Press, 2007.

Parham, Jerrill. *Thrills and Spills: Fast Sports*. Shockwave Social Studies. New York: Children's Press/Scholastic, 2008.

Tibballs, Geoff. *Ripley's Believe it or Not: Twists Sports*. Orlando, Fla.: Ripley Pub., 2010.

INTERNET SITES

FactHound offers a safe, fun way to find Internet sites related to this book. All of the sites on FactHound have been researched by our staff.

Here's all you do:

Visit *www.facthound.com*

FactHound will fetch the best sites for you!

INDEX